AL LEONARD

# HARMONICA FOR KIDS

### A Beginner's Guide with Step-by-Step Instruction for Diatonic Harmonica

### BY ERIC PLAHNA

To access audio visit:
**www.halleonard.com/mylibrary**

Enter Code
2724-0682-0540-0061

ISBN 978-1-4803-9798-9

HAL•LEONARD®
CORPORATION

7777 W. BLUEMOUND RD. P.O. BOX 13819 MILWAUKEE, WI 53213

Visit Hal Leonard Online at
**www.halleonard.com**

# SELECTING YOUR HARMONICA

There are many different kinds and sizes of harmonicas.

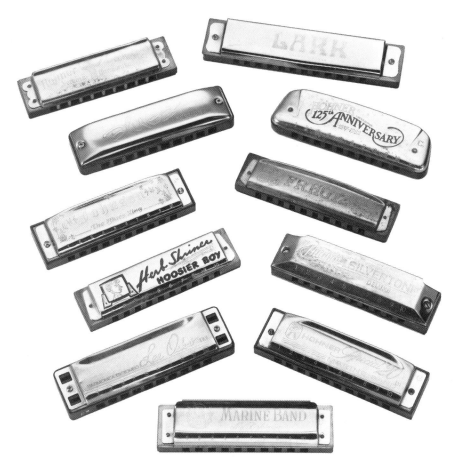

The kind of harmonica we will use for this book is the most common: the 10-hole diatonic harmonica in the key of C. There is no need to buy an expensive harmonica. The reliable and inexpensive Hohner Pocket Pal or Hohner Old Standby is recommended, but any 10-hole diatonic harmonica in the key of C will do. Just make sure that the harmonica you are using has a single row of 10 holes and is marked with the letter "C."

*The Hohner "Old Standby" and "Pocket Pal"*

# HOLDING THE HARMONICA

The correct way to hold the harmonica is between the thumb and first finger of your left hand, with the holes facing you and the numbers on top, like this (if you are left-handed, just reverse these instructions):

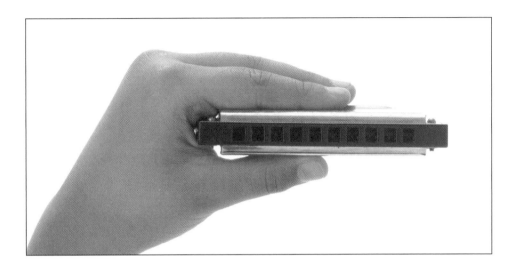

Now place your right hand like this:

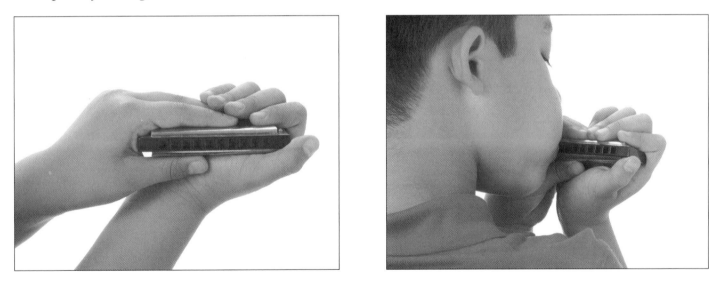

This is one of the better ways to hold a harmonica, but you may hold it any way you like. Just remember that the numbers should be on top and your hands should not interfere with your lips or jaw.

# FIRST SOUNDS

Put your mouth anywhere on the holes of the harmonica and blow gently; then draw or suck air through the same holes. If you blow or draw on more than two holes at the same time, you are playing a **chord**. A chord is more than two notes played at the same time. Experiment by playing three holes at the same time. Focus on making the best quality sound you can while blowing and also drawing.

# READING HARMONICA MUSIC

One way to read harmonica music is by using **standard notation**. Another way is by using the **number/arrow system**.

The number/arrow system, or **tablature**, is easy to learn. The number tells you which hole or holes to use, and the arrow tells you whether to blow or draw. The chart below tells you the name of the note you're playing when you blow or draw on a certain numbered hole. Arrow up ↑ means blow, arrow down ↓ means draw.

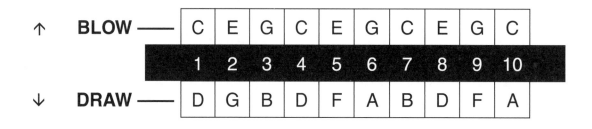

This tablature, or **tab**, $\begin{smallmatrix}5\\4\\3\end{smallmatrix}\uparrow$, tells you to blow on the 3, 4, and 5 holes at the same time.

This tab, $\begin{smallmatrix}5\\4\\3\end{smallmatrix}\downarrow$, means to draw on the 3, 4, and 5 holes at the same time. Now try playing these in the following exercise. Blow or draw once each time you see a chord.

# DRAWING AND BLOWING EXERCISE 🔊

Bar lines divide music into measures.                    A double bar line means the end.

After you play it, listen to the demo to hear if you played it correctly.

To make sure you are using the correct holes, you can check by using your thumbs to block the holes on either side of the note or notes you wish to play.

With just these two chords, play this simple version of the tune "Mary Had a Little Lamb" using the tablature below:

# MARY HAD A LITTLE LAMB — Simple Chords 🔊

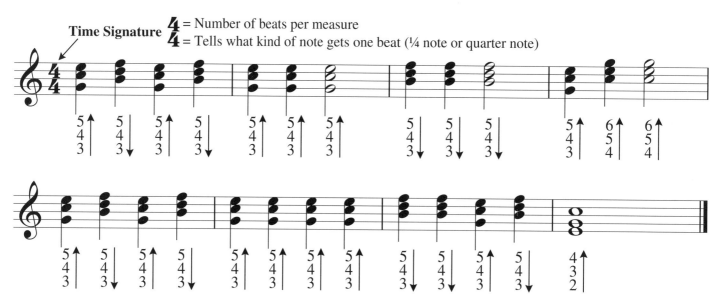

Here is "Mary Had a Little Lamb," written in standard notation with tablature. Notice that two new chords, $\frac{6}{5}$ and $\frac{4}{3}$, have been added to make it sound better than the simple version above. Read the tab under the notes to play the tune. After you play "Mary Had a Little Lamb," more will be explained about standard notation. In this book we will use both the number/arrow system (tablature) and standard notation.

# MARY HAD A LITTLE LAMB — Chords 🔊

Listen to the demo to hear it played, and then try the slow play-along. You will hear four clicks, or beats, at the **tempo** (speed) of the song before the music starts. After you can play the slow version pretty well, try the normal play-along.

# STANDARD NOTATION

With standard notation, music is written on a **staff** of five lines and four spaces. Each line and space on a staff has a letter name. A **clef** appears at the beginning of every staff. Harmonica music is written using the **treble clef**.

Music has a steady beat, like the ticking of a clock. A **quarter note** (♩) gets one of those ticks (or beats), a **half note** (♩) gets two beats, and a **whole note** (**o**) gets four beats.

Here is another tune using the same four chords plus two more: $\frac{4}{3}\big\downarrow$ and $\frac{6}{5}\big\downarrow$ . Notice there are **ledger lines** in this next song. The highest note of the $\frac{6}{5}\big\downarrow$ chord is above the staff. Ledger lines show where the notes are when written above or below the staff. There will be higher ledger lines and lower ledger lines used in songs later in the book.

# TWINKLE, TWINKLE LITTLE STAR — Chords 🔊

Remember, learning any musical instrument takes time! Do the best you can on each song before moving to the next one.

# PLAYING SINGLE NOTES

To play single notes, think of puckering your lips to whistle, or blowing or sucking through a soda straw. First, practice playing some single notes until they sound clear, then play "Mary Had a Little Lamb" reading the notes and tablature below.

## MARY HAD A LITTLE LAMB — Single Notes

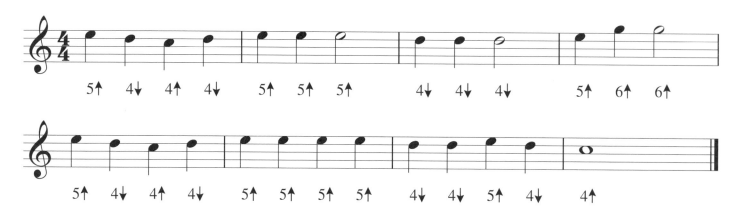

Now, learn "Twinkle, Twinkle Little Star" with single notes.

## TWINKLE, TWINKLE LITTLE STAR — Single Notes

With the song "Jingle Bells," learn the single-note version first.

# JINGLE BELLS – Single Notes

# JINGLE BELLS – Chords

All the songs for the rest of the book will be written with single notes only. Experiment with the songs by playing them with chords also. Many of them will sound great. "Camptown Races" is an easy song to try that out. To help you get started, there is a demo recording included with a chord version of the tune.

## DOTTED NOTES

A **dot** next to a note makes the note longer by half. So, if there is a dot on a half note (two beats), the dot is worth half of two beats, or 1 beat.

2+1=3        A dotted half note ($\sJ\,.$) is worth three beats.

# CAMPTOWN RACES

Up to now, we have had played songs with four beats in each measure, or 4/4 time. "Blow the Man Down" has three beats per measure. This is called **3/4 time**.

# BLOW THE MAN DOWN

You'll see **chord symbols** in the following song. This tells other instruments (like piano or guitar) what chord to play along with our harmonica part. When you see chord symbols in this book, they're for the teacher (or maybe a friend who plays guitar or piano) to play.

# GO TELL AUNT RHODY

# ITSY BITSY SPIDER

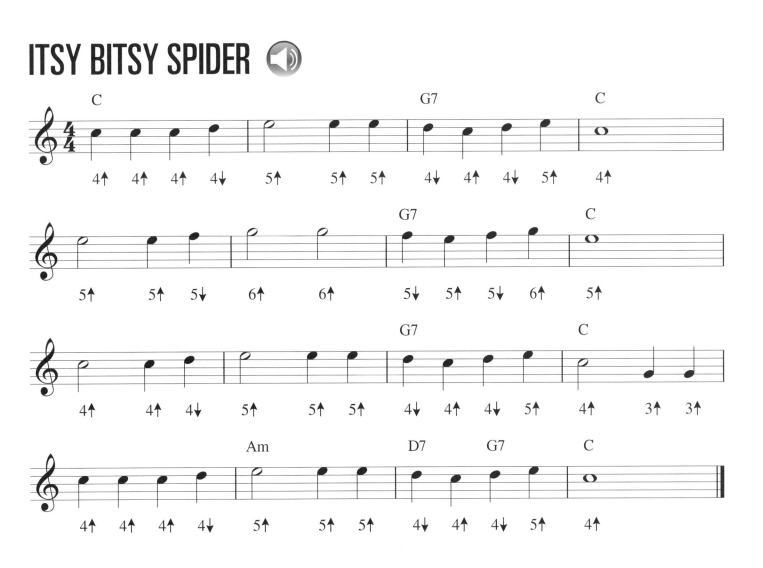

# SONG OF THE VOLGA BOATMAN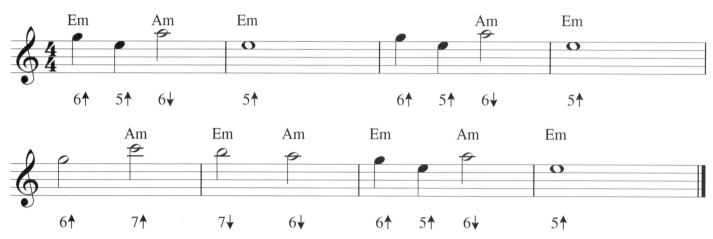

**TEACHER ACCOMPANIMENT:**

# LOVE ME TENDER

Words and Music by
Elvis Presley and Vera Matson

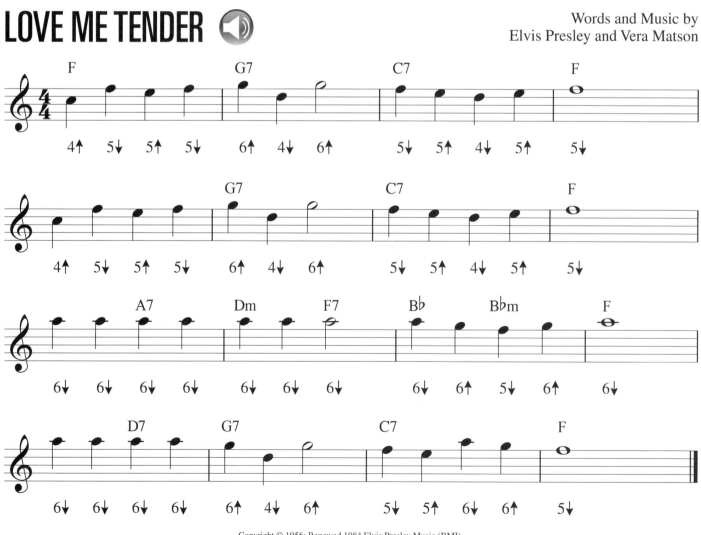

## PICKUP NOTES

Sometimes songs start with only part of a measure. The note or notes in that incomplete measure are called **pickup notes**.

On the recordings for "The Streets of Laredo," you will hear five clicks before the song begins: three beats for a complete measure, and then two more for the incomplete measure, where the pickup note starts it off.

# THE STREETS OF LAREDO 🔊

# TIES

A **tie** connects two or more notes to create one longer note.

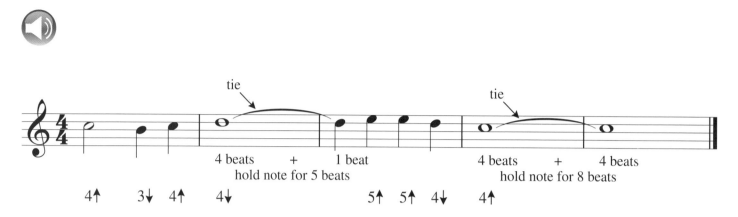

"You Are My Sunshine" includes ties and also three pickup notes. The recording will begin with five clicks—four beats for a full measure and one for the incomplete measure.

# YOU ARE MY SUNSHINE

Words and Music by
Jimmie Davis

# RESTS

**Rests** are the sound of silence. The **quarter rest** (𝄽) tells you to be silent for one beat.

The **half rest** ( ▬ ) tells you to be silent for two beats. And the **whole rest** ( ▬ ) tells you to be silent for the whole measure.

# WHEN THE SAINTS GO MARCHING IN

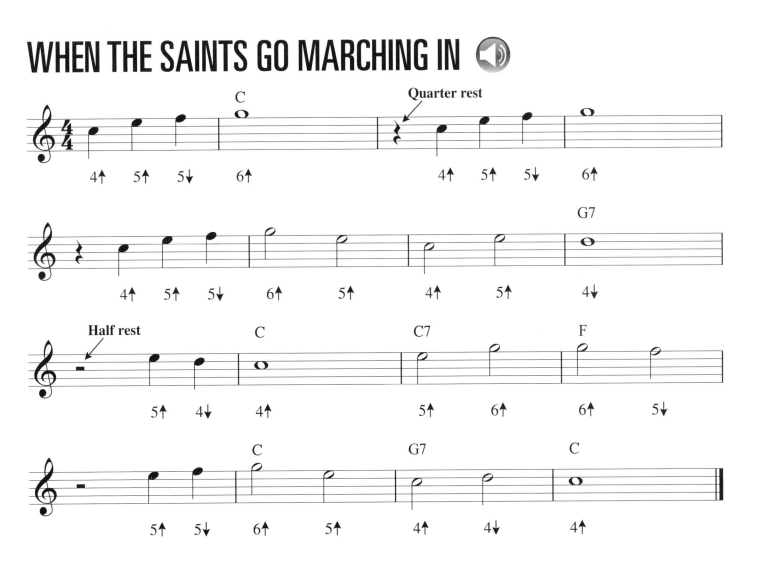

**TEACHER ACCOMPANIMENT:**

# ROW, ROW, ROW YOUR BOAT

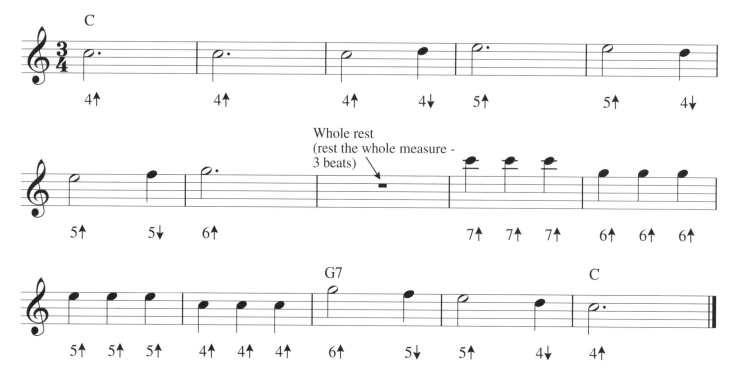

## OCTAVES

You might have noticed that there are several notes on the harmonica that have the same letter name, such as the note C. The C notes at holes 1, 4, 7, and 10 are all the same note, but are simply higher or lower in sound. The distance between each of these notes is called an **octave**. Try playing each C note to hear how they are different and the same.

# HARMONICA SONGS

The next section of this book contains many fun songs to practice and play. Some of these songs use very high notes (holes 8 to 10). It is a little harder to make a good sound with high notes. If you blow or draw too hard or too soft they don't sound as good. Practice to get the best sound possible. For some of the songs with high notes, we have written the notes lower because too many ledger lines are harder to read. Those songs will have "Written one octave lower" above the first measure. The tablature remains the same.

## WHEN JOHNNY COMES MARCHING HOME

# SCARBOROUGH FAIR

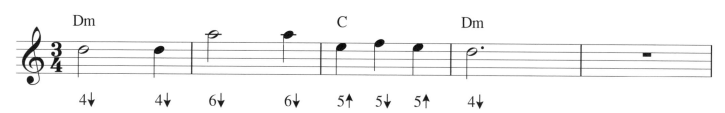

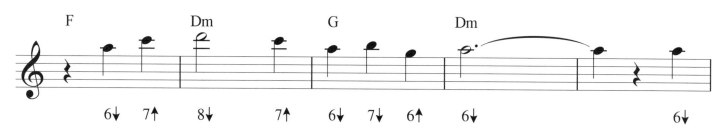

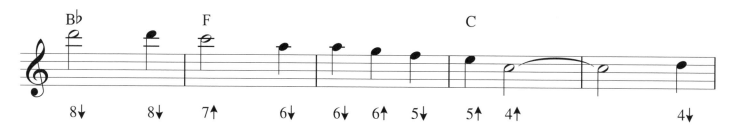

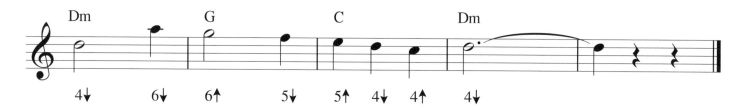

# ON TOP OF OLD SMOKY

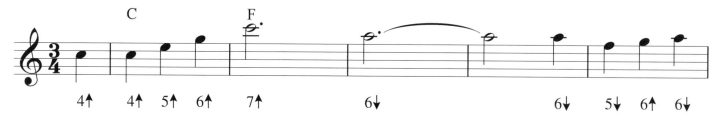

# HEIGH-HO

Words by Larry Morey
Music by Frank Churchill

Copyright © 1937 by Bourne Co. (ASCAP)
Copyright Renewed
International Copyright Secured  All Rights Reserved

# DOWN IN THE VALLEY

Remember to listen to the demos to get a feel for the melodies.

# THE RED RIVER VALLEY

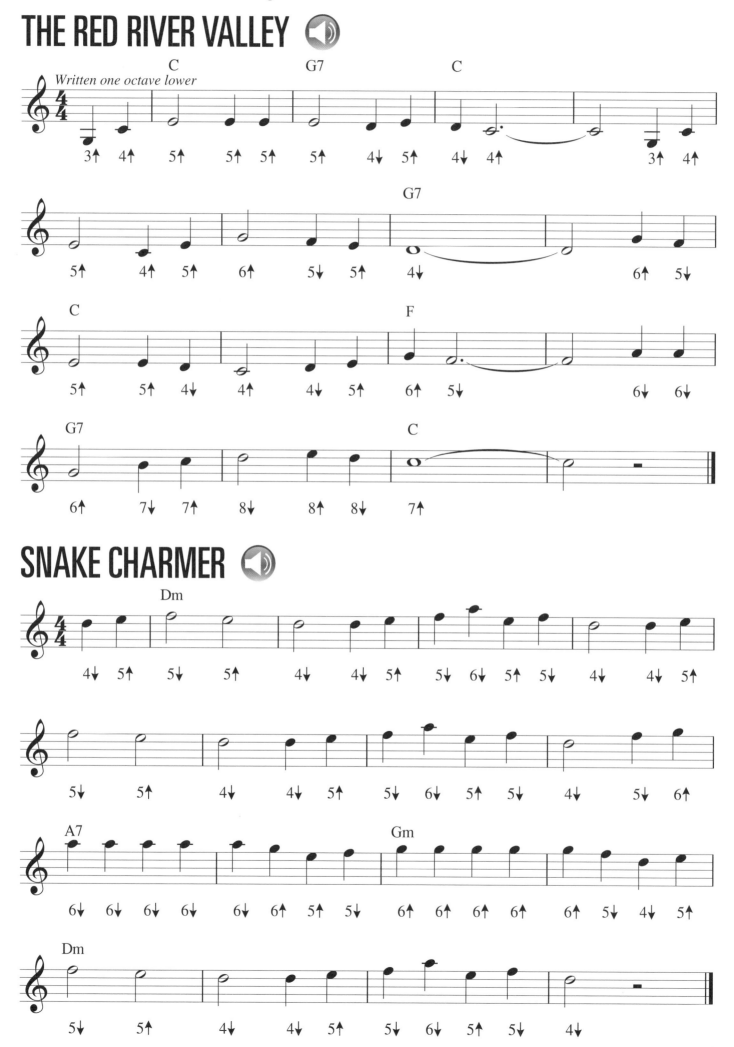

# SNAKE CHARMER

Remember to stop playing during the rests in the music. They can be just as important as the notes themselves!

# TAKE ME OUT TO THE BALL GAME

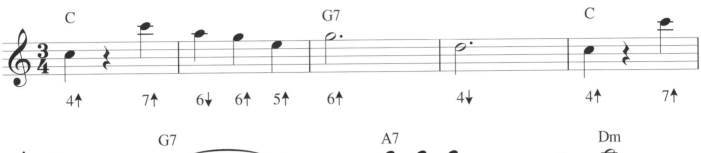

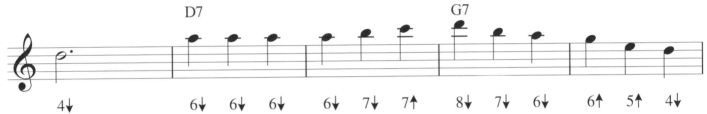

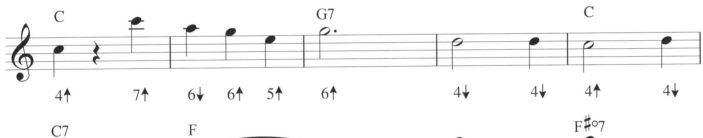

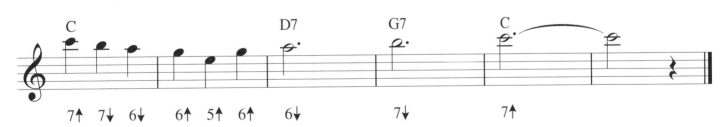

# YANKEE DOODLE

# BINGO

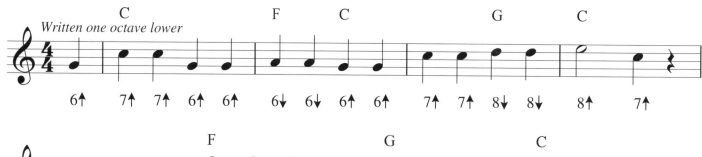

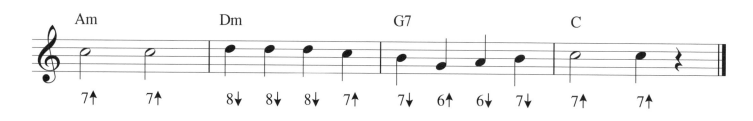

## COUNTING

If you're having trouble reading rhythms, try counting and clapping through a song before you play it. For example, in the next song you would count "1, 2, 3, 1, 2, 3" for each beat of the 3/4 time signature while clapping once for each note.

# OVER THE RIVER AND THROUGH THE WOODS

# WHEN IRISH EYES ARE SMILING

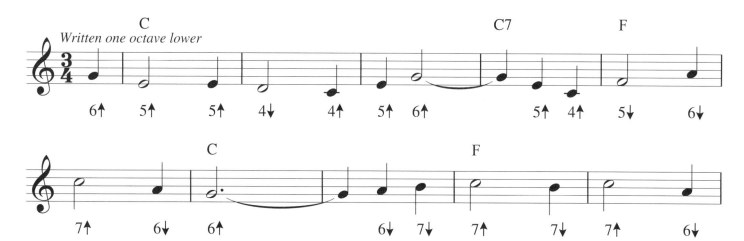

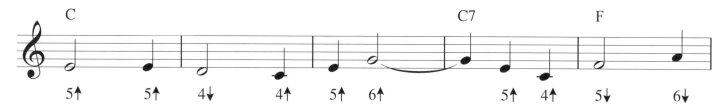

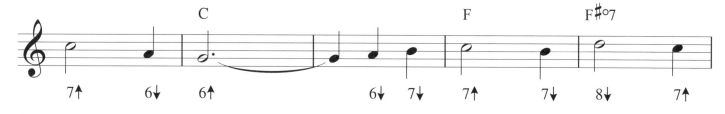

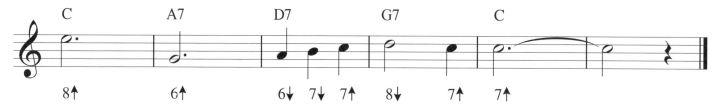

# IT'S A SMALL WORLD

Words and Music by
Richard M. Sherman and Robert B. Sherman

Notice the **fermata** over the last note of this song. This symbol tells you to hold the note a little longer than usual.

# LONDONDERRY AIR (DANNY BOY)

## EIGHTH NOTES

An **eighth note** has one flag ♪. Two or more eighth notes are connected by a beam ♫. The value of an eighth note is half of a quarter note (or half of a beat), so it takes two eighth notes to equal one quarter note. Listen to the demo of the next song to hear this rhythm.

# SKIP TO MY LOU

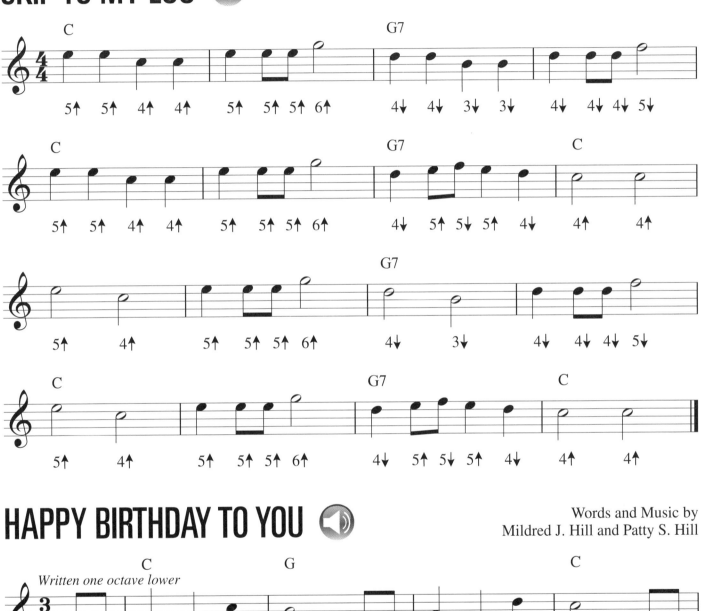

# HAPPY BIRTHDAY TO YOU

Words and Music by
Mildred J. Hill and Patty S. Hill

# EDELWEISS

Lyrics by Oscar Hammerstein II
Music by Richard Rodgers

"Oh! Susanna" sounds especially good played with chords. Give it a try after you learn the single-note melody.

# OH! SUSANNA

# THIS OLD MAN

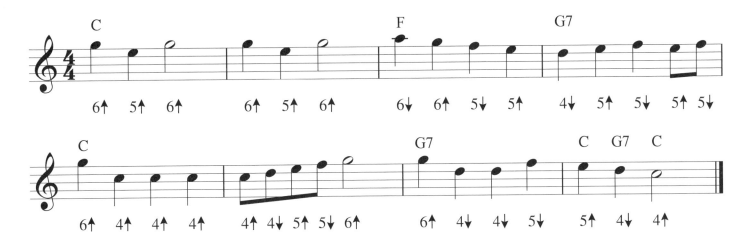

# ALL MY LOVING

Words and Music by
John Lennon and Paul McCartney

# THIS LAND IS YOUR LAND

Words and Music by
Woody Guthrie

There are many different kinds of **scales**, but C major is probably the most common. Your harmonica is a C major harmonica. Here is the C major scale written with eighth notes, going up and back down.

# C MAJOR SCALE

| do | re | mi | fa | sol | la | ti | do | do | ti | la | sol | fa | mi | re | do |
|----|----|----|----|-----|----|----|----|----|----|----|-----|----|----|----|----|
| C  | D  | E  | F  | G   | A  | B  | C  | C  | B  | A  | G   | F  | E  | D  | C  |

4↑  4↓  5↑  5↓  6↑  6↓  7↓  7↑   7↑  7↓  6↓  6↑  5↓  5↑  4↓  4↑

An **arpeggio** is a chord whose notes are played separately.

# ARPEGGIO

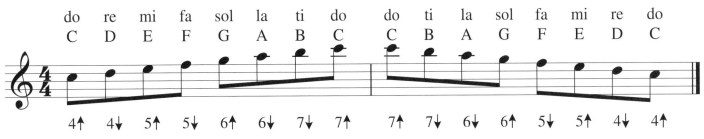

The words to the song from the movie, *The Aristocats*, explain how important scales and arpeggios are!

# SCALES AND ARPEGGIOS

Words and Music by
Richard M. Sherman and Robert B. Sherman

If you're faithful to your daily practicing,
you will find your progress is encouraging.
Do mi so mi, do mi so mi, fa la so it goes,
when you do your scales and your arpeggios.

Though at first it seems as though it doesn't show,
like a tree, ability will bloom and grow.
If you're smart, you'll learn by heart what every artist knows,
you must sing your scales and your arpeggios.

**TEACHER ACCOMPANIMENT:**